BIOGRAPHIES

FRANKLIN D. ROOSEVELT

by Laura K. Murray

PEBBLE
a capstone imprint

Pebble Explore is published by Pebble, an imprint of Capstone.
1710 Roe Crest Drive
North Mankato, Minnesota 56003
www.capstonepub.com

Library of Congress Cataloging-in-Publication data is available on the Library of Congress website.
ISBN: 978-1-9771-1358-0 (library binding)
ISBN: 978-1-9771-1802-8 (paperback)
ISBN: 978-1-9771-1366-5 (eBook PDF)

Summary: Explores the life, challenges, and accomplishments of Franklin D. Roosevelt, the 32nd president of the United States.

Image Credits
FDR Presidential Library & Museum: cover, 1, 5, 6, 10, 11, 14, 16, 18, 19, 21, 22, 27, 29; Getty Images: WireImage/John Lamparski, 26; Library of Congress: 9, 13; Newscom: akg-images, 17, Everett Collection, 23; Shutterstock: Curly Pat (geometric background), cover, back cover, 2, 29, Jeffrey M. Frank, 24, lunamarina, 25; U.S. Navy: 20; Wikimedia: Tennessee Valley Authority, 12

Editorial Credits
Christopher Harbo, editor; Elyse White, designer; Svetlana Zhurkin, media researcher; Katy LaVigne, production specialist

Printed and bound in China.
2489

Table of Contents

Who Was Franklin D. Roosevelt? 4

Growing Up Franklin 6

A Hopeful Leader 10

Family and Hobbies 16

The World at War 20

Remembering FDR 24

Important Dates 28

Fast Facts 29

Glossary 30

Read More 31

Internet Sites 31

Index 32

Words in **bold** are in the glossary.

Who Was Franklin D. Roosevelt?

Franklin D. Roosevelt was the 32nd **president** of the United States. He was president four times in a row. That was the most of any president! Franklin led the United States through hard times. He was president when many people couldn't find jobs or pay their bills. He also led the country through war.

Franklin is often called "FDR." He gave people hope and put the United States on a good path. His new ideas changed the country forever.

Growing Up Franklin

Franklin D. Roosevelt was born January 30, 1882, in Hyde Park, New York. As a boy, he played outside on the land around his family's home. He went on trips to Europe too.

Franklin in 1889

Teachers came to Franklin's home until he was 14. Then he lived at a **boarding school**. Next Franklin went to college at Harvard University. He ran the school's newspaper.

After college, he became a **lawyer**. He helped other people understand the law, but he did not like the work.

Theodore Roosevelt was the 26th U.S. president. Franklin was Theodore's distant cousin. Franklin looked up to him. Franklin wanted to work in government too.

Franklin became a New York state **senator** in 1910. He helped pass laws to keep forests and animals safe. He later worked for the U.S. Navy.

Franklin got **polio** in 1921 when he was 39. The disease hurt the muscles in his legs. After that, he had to use a wheelchair.

Franklin at work for the Navy in 1913

A Hopeful Leader

Franklin was **elected** the **governor** of New York in 1928. The next year the **Great Depression** hit the country. Many people lost money when banks closed. Many also lost their jobs. Franklin started programs to get people back to work.

Franklin as governor in 1931

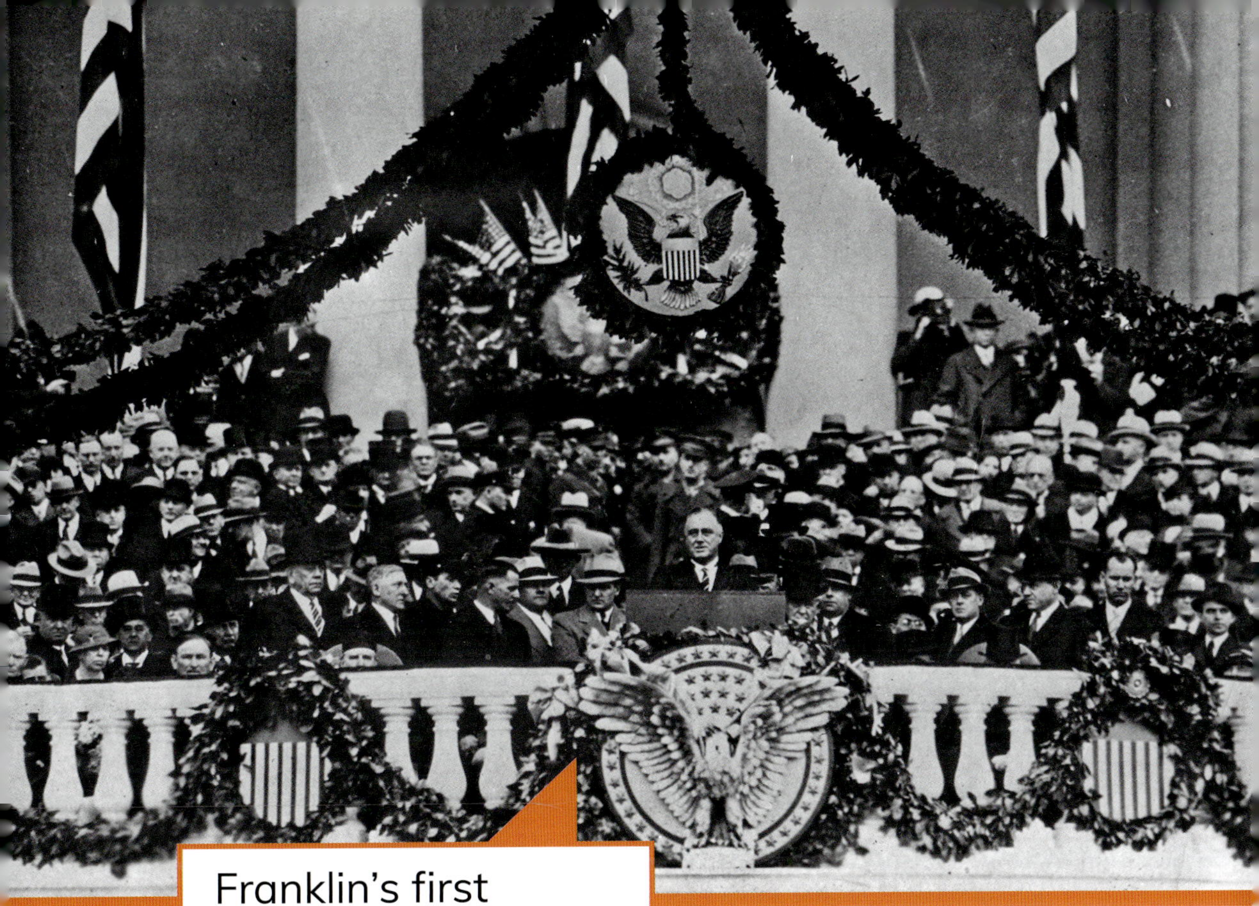

Franklin's first speech as president

Franklin decided to run for president. He had a plan to help the country. He called it the "New Deal." Franklin was elected president in 1932 at age 50. In his first speech, he told the country not to be afraid.

Franklin signed an act that gave people jobs in 1933.

Franklin got a lot done in his first 100 days as president. He started new programs to get the country back on track. Some programs helped the poor. Others helped banks and farmers.

Franklin's programs gave jobs to men and women. People planted trees and fought forest fires. They built roads, bridges, and dams. The Great Depression lasted until 1939. But Franklin kept working to help families.

Hoover Dam being built in 1934

Franklin talked
on the radio.

In the 1930s, most people owned a radio. In 1933, Franklin began talking about his ideas on the radio. Many people thought Franklin sounded friendly and wise. They felt like Franklin was talking right to them. His talks were called fireside chats.

Franklin was elected president for a second time in 1936 at age 54. He won every state except two. In 1940, Franklin was elected president for a third time!

Family and Hobbies

Franklin had a large family. Franklin married Eleanor Roosevelt in 1905 at age 23. They had one daughter and five sons. Eleanor helped take care of Franklin when he got polio.

Franklin with his family in 1916

Eleanor Roosevelt talked on the radio.

The country had never had a first lady like Eleanor. She had her own radio show. She met with leaders and became known all over the world.

Franklin with his stamp collection

Franklin had many hobbies. He liked fishing, horseback riding, sailing, and swimming. Franklin began keeping stamps as a boy. When he got polio, he gathered even more stamps. His collection grew to more than 1 million stamps!

Franklin got a dog named Fala in 1940. He was a black Scottish terrier. Fala lived at the White House. He was never far from Franklin's side. Fala was so popular that people sent him letters.

Franklin with Fala and a young girl in Hyde Park

The World at War

On December 7, 1941, Japan attacked the U.S. Navy at Pearl Harbor in Hawaii. The United States entered World War II (1939–1945). It joined Great Britain and other countries. They fought Germany, Italy, and Japan.

Pearl Harbor attack

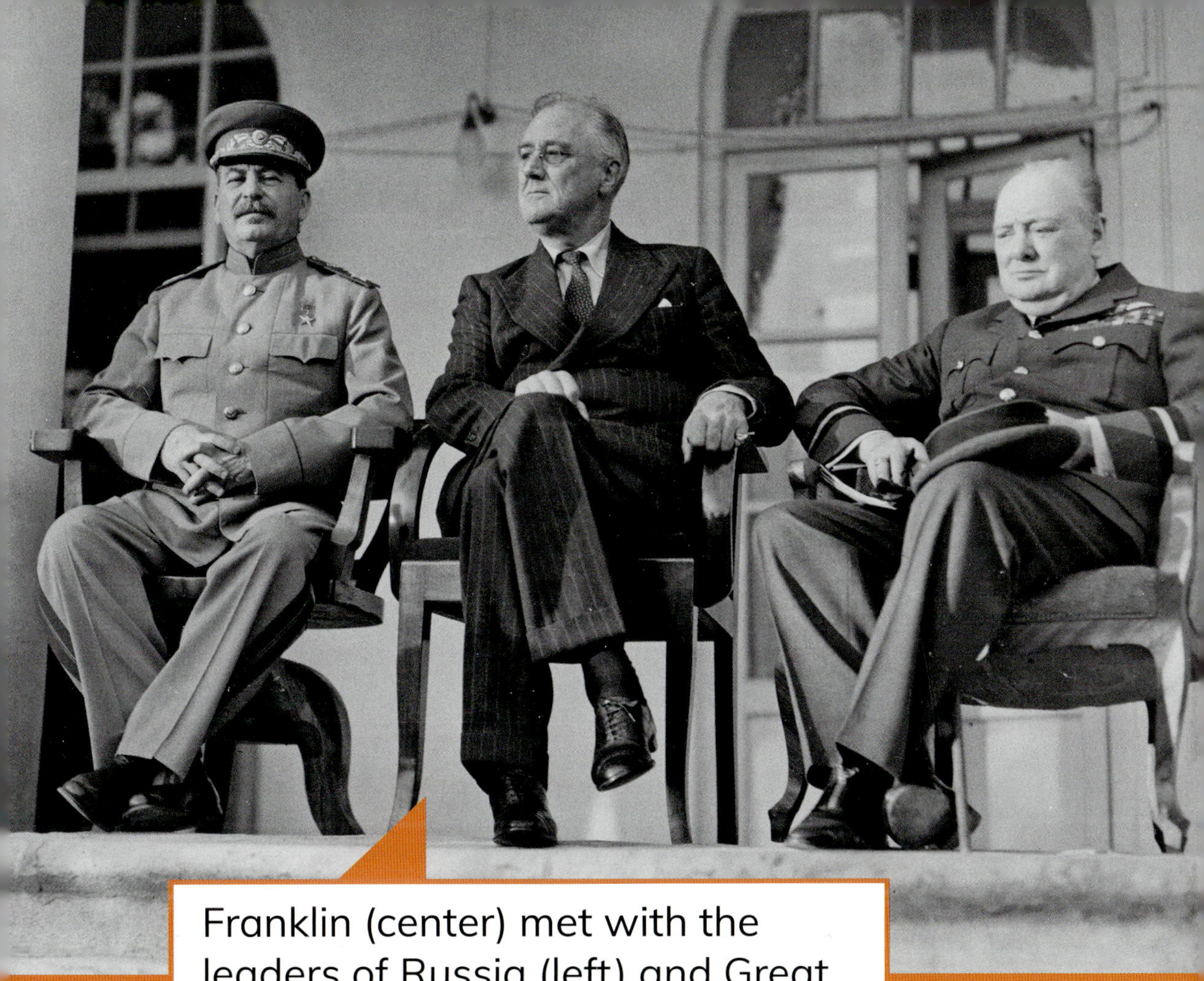

Franklin (center) met with the leaders of Russia (left) and Great Britain (right) during World War II.

During the war, Franklin met with world leaders. They made plans to form a new group. It would help keep freedom and peace in the world. Later the group became the **United Nations**.

Franklin ran for president in 1944.

Franklin was elected president for a fourth time in 1944 at age 62. But the next year, sickness made him weaker. He went to rest at his home in Warm Springs, Georgia. It was called the Little White House. He did not get better. Franklin died on April 12, 1945, at age 63.

The world was shocked. Many people lined up to see the wagon that carried his body. Franklin was buried in Hyde Park, New York.

Franklin's funeral parade

Remembering FDR

Today people can see important places in Franklin's life. Each year more than 100,000 people go to Franklin's childhood home in New York. It has a museum and a library.

Franklin's childhood home

FDR Memorial

In Washington, D.C., people visit the FDR **Memorial**. They walk through four outdoor rooms. Waterfalls run down the stone walls. Statues show Franklin, Eleanor, and their dog, Fala.

Many of Franklin's programs still help people today. In 1938, Franklin started a program to help children with polio. Now it is called the March of Dimes. It helps mothers and babies. Franklin's face is on the U.S. dime to honor this work.

The world changed a lot when Franklin D. Roosevelt was president. He led the country through hard times and tried new ideas. He helped people believe that things would get better. He showed them how to have hope.

Important Dates

January 30, 1882	Franklin D. Roosevelt is born in Hyde Park, New York.
March 17, 1905	Franklin marries Eleanor Roosevelt.
November 8, 1910	Franklin is elected a New York state senator.
August 1921	Franklin gets a disease called polio.
November 6, 1928	Franklin becomes the governor of New York.
November 8, 1932	Franklin is elected president of the United States.
March 12, 1933	Franklin gives his first fireside chat on the radio.
November 3, 1936	Franklin is elected president of the United States for a second time.
November 5, 1940	Franklin is elected president of the United States for a third time.
November 7, 1944	Franklin is elected president of the United States for a fourth time.
April 12, 1945	Franklin dies at age 63.

Fast Facts

Name:
Franklin D. Roosevelt

Role:
32nd president of the United States

Life dates:
January 30, 1882 to April 12, 1945

Key accomplishments:
Franklin D. Roosevelt was the 32nd president of the United States. He was elected four times and created the New Deal programs that helped the country during the Great Depression. Franklin also led the United States through World War II.

Glossary

boarding school (BOR-ding SKOOL)—a school where students live during the school year

elected (i-LEKT-ed)—to be chosen as a leader by voting

governor (GUHV-urn-ur)—a person elected to lead a state's government

Great Depression (GRAYT di-PRESH-uhn)—the years from 1929 to 1939, when there were few jobs and most people had little money or food

lawyer (LAW-yur)—a person who is trained to advise people about the law

memorial (muh-MOR-ee-uhl)—something that is built or done to help people remember a person or event

polio (POH-lee-oh)—a disease that attacks the nerves, spinal cord, and brain

president (PREZ-uh-duhnt)—the highest elected job in a class, business, or country

senator (SEN-ah-tur)—a person elected to represent the people in the government

United Nations (yoo-NI-ted NAY-shuns)—a group of countries that work together for peace and security

Read More

Gregory, Josh. *Franklin D. Roosevelt: The 32nd President*. New York: Bearport Publishing, 2015.

Rajczak, Michael. *Before Franklin D. Roosevelt Was President*. New York: Gareth Stevens Publishing, 2019.

Roome, Hugh. *Franklin D. Roosevelt: American Hero*. New York: Children's Press, 2018.

Internet Sites

FDR Presidential Library and Museum
https://fdrlibrary.org/home

Franklin D. Roosevelt
https://www.whitehouse.gov/about-the-white-house/presidents/franklin-d-roosevelt/

Home of Franklin D. Roosevelt
https://www.nps.gov/nr/travel/presidents/fdr_home.html

Index

birth, 6, 28, 29

childhood home, 6, 24

death, 22–23, 28, 29

education, 7

Fala, 19, 25
family, 16–17
fireside chats, 15, 28

governor, 10, 28
Great Depression, 10, 13, 29

hobbies, 18

jobs, 4, 7, 8, 10, 13

March of Dimes, 26
memorials, 25

New Deal, 11, 29
nickname, 4

polio, 8, 16, 18, 26, 28
president, 4, 8, 11, 12–13, 15, 22, 27, 28, 29

Roosevelt, Eleanor, 16–17, 25, 28
Roosevelt, Theodore, 8

senator, 8, 28

United Nations, 21

World War II, 20–21, 29